Anonymous

**House Painting**

Anonymous

**House Painting**

ISBN/EAN: 9783337817763

Printed in Europe, USA, Canada, Australia, Japan

Cover: Foto ©ninafisch / pixelio.de

More available books at **www.hansebooks.com**

# HOUSE

## PAINTING

# 1899

F. W. DEVOE & COMPANY

NEW YORK AND CHICAGO

# THE SKIMMER

Sometimes a reader likes to skim over a book, pick out the nicest parts, and read them first; then, if he thinks it worth his while, begin at the beginning and take it all in.

The prettiest nugget, in this, is a practical joke by a painter in Paris fifty years ago. He got a Gold Medal and the Grand Cross of the Legion of Honor for it. That is on page 31.

# CONTENTS

## I. WHAT PAINT IS FOR

## II. WHAT PAINT SHOULD BE

## III. WHAT PAINT TO USE

# YOU ARE PROBABLY ONE OF 'EM

---

This book is for two sorts of men ; yes, three.

Some think they can't paint, because they have never done such a thing. The book is for them.

Now and then a man feels so cock-sure of whatever he thinks he knows, that people say " he knows it all." It is a sly way of saying " he don't know what an awful lot of things there are in the world that he don't know." There's a little in it for him.

But the bulk of Americans, painters or not, feel able to do a good-enough job with the help of a little schooling. Here's the schooling.

# HOUSE-PAINTING.

## I.

## WHAT PAINT IS FOR.

### A MISTAKE.

As you pass your neighbor's house, if the paint looks fresh and attractive, you say to yourself: "Lucky dog! the market is always on his side." Which means that Jones is a man of good sense. That's what luck is: good sense. Success always comes, if it lasts, of good sense. If his paint is shabby, you say: "Poor fellow! the world is too much for him." *You estimate men by their paint*

Paint is as true a sign, as there is, of thrift and unthrift. Thrift is the habit of doing things that pay; unthrift is the habit of doing the other things. The habit of thrift is the gift of seeing things, as they are, in a good clear light. The unthrifty habit is not being quite sure, and waiting. The man who sees right, and goes quick, is the one who gets there, and takes his choice. The other one takes his time and gets left. Fresh paint is the sign of one; the need of it marks the other. *Men estimate you by your paint*

*Thrift and unthrift*

But this is the poorest reason for painting. If Smith is slack he won't become brisk by *Paint and look prosperous* merely painting his house; if he is behind, it'll take more than paint to set him ahead. It is only a sign of the property-getting and property-keeping faculty; not a begetter of it, or a substitute for it.

**Paint and be prosperous**

The real reason, for painting this year, is not to look prosperous, but to be so. It pays. It pays to look prosperous too, but to be so first. If your house and outbuildings and fences are cheerful and bright, you have done your best for both your estate and your standing.

**The mistake**

What mistake do we mean, then? It is thinking of paint as a luxury. That is the poorest recommendation for it.

**The fact**

Paint is a small and safe investment, bearing a high rate of interest.

## HOME AND BUSINESS HOME.

**One's most precious property**

The most precious property anyone has is his domestic home, and the next is his business home. A farmer's business home is the rest of his buildings; a merchant's his store; a mechanic's his shop.

**Object of life and dearer than life**

The house, that shelters his business, made and sustains his domestic home.

**But perishable**

It is built of wood, and stands in sunshine, dew and rain, subject to decay, unless protected with paint.

## FRIENDS AND ENEMIES.

**Paint keeps wood as salt keeps meat**

Dry wood, in our part of the world, keeps sound and whole, till rotted with water or burnt with fire. We insure against water by paint; against fire, by sharing our losses with others.

Rain beats on and into the roof and sides, soaks in, runs down, backs up, and streams in. Snow stops the eaves, and the melting of snow is worse than the beating of rain. Dew steals in while we are asleep; and the sun, in the morning, steams it out. Perhaps dew, that we do not think of as injuring wood, is worse than storms; because it is busy all the time. *Water in every form*

We are always in danger of water; fire, we hope to avoid. We keep the first enemy out with paint; if the other gets in, insurance pays part of the damage. *Water-insurance*

### THE PRINCIPAL USE OF PAINT.

A good enough reason for painting, indoors or out, is for looks; but the great big reason indoors, as women know best, is to save nine-tenths of the labor of keeping the house in a decent condition of cleanliness; outdoors, to keep wood from rotting, and iron from rusting. *Indoors and outdoors*

We paint indoors for cleanliness, brightness and beauty. *Saves labor*

We paint outdoors to resist the weather, to protect the building, and to make it last. *Saves loss*

The real use of paint, then—its use to every man who owns a house—is to save expense and loss. *Expense and loss*

## BE GENEROUS WITH IT.

Be generous
with it

Paint is a money and property saver, not an expense. Be generous with it. Paint when your property needs it, use good paint, and paint right.

Generosity cheap

But paint and painting are different things. Good painting costs very little more money than poor painting; pay it; be glad to pay it. But you can buy the best of paint for less money than some poor paint. High cost is no sign of goodness; low cost is no sign of cheapness.

## A, B, C.

Begin at the
beginning

If you have read so far, you are on your way to a knowledge of painting and paint that few of us really have; and you have some clue to the rest of the book. We shall offer you nothing but what you need, to do good work: to paint intelligently: one thing at a time in the easiest order: the a b c of the business. The a b c is the most important part of anything. Get the right start.

# II

# WHAT PAINT SHOULD BE.

## WATERPROOF.

The business of paint is to turn water. Good paint turns water. It keeps wood from rotting, and iron from rusting, by turning water. To turn water, it must have no hole in it, no spongy places.

One coat of paint is sure to have imperfections in it; so we put on two coats. Two coats may have imperfections, so we put on three. The three unite to form one. There is not likely to be a hole or spongy part in this thick coat consisting of three successive thin ones.

## DURABLE.

That is not the whole of the reason for painting three coats: to have no hole in the paint. The rest of the reason is that paint wears out; we want it thick, to *last*.

Each coat must be thin, to dry; not merely to dry outside, on top, but to dry through and underneath as well as on top, to make a uniform coat all through; so that when the three coats unite to form one, that one shall be dry all through, and of one uniform substance all through.

Paint is a rubbery coat of oil and pigment.*

*Marginal notes:* Turn water — No hole in it — Hence three thin coats — to form one thick one — Thick to wear — Thin to dry — One uniform substance all through — Thick, rubbery coat

* Pigment means the solid part of paint, the part not liquid. Remember the word; we shall use it again.

The oil for a durable rubbery coat is linseed; the pigments are various. Every part must be right, to make durable paint; and the market is full of inferior stuff with superior names, to cover adulterations and substitutions.

*Fine feathers don't make fine birds*

*Adulterants*

The genuine things can be got; but they cost a certain amount of money. The false pretend to be true; cost less; and commonly pass for true, with people who buy cheap stuff. It is easy, you see, for a man who mixes his own paint to use wrong materials. And, if he buys his paint ready-made, there are good and bad ready-made paints, as well as good and bad paint materials.

*Durability first*

Good means durable; bad means something wrong; but good means durable only, no more. When we say good paint, we mean paint that turns water this year, next year, and next after that: we mean durable waterproof paint, no matter about the color. The goodness of paint is its durability, not its color.

*Color next*

Color comes next: it is a totally different subject: important enough in its way; but its way is not wear of paint or turning of water.

## BEAUTIFUL.

*May as well look good, too*

Paint may as well be agreeable too; this depends altogether on color.

*A matter of taste*

Houses used to be painted white, inside and out, with green blinds. We all agree now that white is too bright. It was a natural thing to do, in pioneer times, when painted houses were rare, to make them conspicuous. White is the most conspicuous paint; and the greener we are, the more we go to extremes. A Fiji Islander, having our houses and paint, might paint everything purple and green. Which is worse than white.

A civilized man, especially woman, considers several things besides the sensation of seeing a color or colors together. The choice of colors belongs to taste; but taste considers the circumstances. A color that suits a flower, or a woman's dress, may not suit a house; a color that suits a grand house, may not suit a modest one ; and a color that suits a conspicuous house, may not suit one in a sheltered position. *Consider the circumstances*

It is usual, now, to paint two or three colors: The body of some light tint, and the trim a harmonious solid color.* There is a fashion in house paint, as in everything else ; but, generally, it keeps within the limits of suitableness and economy. Women generally have better color-sense than men ; and no one can put color-sense into or get it out of a book. It is greatly a matter of personal taste. *The fashion*

## CHEAP.

There is a beautiful color, ultramarine, that *Absurd*

* Solid color means, in the language of painters, a color full strength: one to which no white has been added. A tint is a color reduced by white.

costs about twice its weight in gold; of course, it is not much used in any sort of painting. Cadmium yellow, that costs $5 a pound is sparingly used in carriage-painting, not in house-painting. Paris-green costs little enough, by the pound, but is so transparent that several coats are required; which costs too much for house-painting. We make of it nearly a million pounds a year, to kill potato-bugs with; but sell very little for paint. It is an exquisite paint for blinds, when properly applied, but rather impracticable, on account of the cost of putting on many coats.

It is nothing against a paint to say it is low priced. One might, with equal reason, object to fire-insurance, because the premium is low; we get it as low as we can.

The gist of this chapter, so far, is this: the first cost of a house-paint has got to be low, or it will not be used. Which is right and true. It is, however, only half of the truth. You knew it before; we might have left it out. The other half is important because you don't know it. A book that tells what you knew before, is of no account; you want something new.

But there is a difficulty in telling you what you don't know already: you won't believe it. And yet what books are for is to tell what you don't know. If you read nothing but what you know, you don't learn anything.

*Margin notes:* Ditto — Impracticable — It has got to be cheap — Plainer — Commonplace — Something new — You won't believe it — What books are for

The important half of this chapter is not so familiar: the cost of a paint is only one part of its being cheap; the other part is *how long is it going to last.*

Here it is

You may happen to know it; nine-tenths of us don't. The tenth, that know it, are well-to-do. Because they distinguish between good-looking things and good ones. Nine-tenths are not well-to-do, because they throw their money away upon gew-gaw things that don't cost much.

The well-to-do and improvident

The cost of painting a house is, say, $20 for paint and $40 for putting it on—the cost, for putting it on, is as much for poor paint as for good. The cost of the whole job is $60: $10 a year, if it lasts six years; $15 a year, if it lasts four years; $30 a year, if it lasts two years; $60 a year, if it lasts one year.

The lesson applied to paint

There is paint that lasts one year; there is paint that lasts six years. The paint, that lasts six years, is cheap: and the paint that lasts one year is dear. A paint that wears out in a year, no matter how little it costs, is not cheap: it is dear.

The lesson is practical

Now you know what we mean by a paint being really cheap: it is paint that costs short and lasts long. Is there any such paint? Yes, there is; but that comes later. Now don't understand that the paint, that costs least, lasts longest. The price of a paint has nothing to do with the wear of it; still there is paint that costs no more, even less,

Stated again

with a caution

than usual paint, and wears twice as long.

A fraud

There is low-price paint, with which the first cost of a job is high : because of some cheating in weight or measure, or because it lacks body,* requires more coats. So the price of a paint in the store has little to do with the cost of your job.

A mistake

There is also paint, the first cost of which is low, which is dear : because it wears out so soon. So the cost of your job has nothing to do with its cheapness or dearness.

Three requirements

And yet the store-price of house-paint must be low, or the paint will not get used ; the first cost of your paint must be fair (not high), or the paint is a fraud ; and the paint must be durable, or there is some mistake on somebody's part.

Go by the last one

Inexperienced people go by store-price ; experienced men, who think they know about paint or business, go by first cost, and plume themselves on their wisdom; those, who really know either paint or business, go by the wear —and they find out.

Cheap

Let us explain the word-meaning of " cheap."

It has four meanings:

(1) well worth its cost
(2) costs little
(3) both (1) and (2)
(4) good-for-nothing

---

* Body means covering-capacity, hiding-capacity, non-transparency ; can't see through the paint.

Our meaning is the third : the less paint costs, and the longer it lasts, the cheaper it is.

But there is such a thing as cheap paint, in the second sense, to the *maker;* and cheap, in the fourth, to the house owner. It is a poverty-breeder. If you are a poor man, we venture to guess the cause : you can't resist the temptation of "cheap" in the second and fourth of those meanings : your money goes for humbugs.

Poverty-breeder

Humbugs as bad as whiskey

Is there anything new, in this chapter, to you ? The paint, that is really cheap, costs less than usual paint, and lasts twice as long : there is such a paint. We told you you wouldn't believe it. Better not read any further, may be. You either see what this book is for, or you don't. It is to teach you paint and economy : paint and prosperity.

Can you take the lesson

# III.

## WHAT PAINT TO USE.

### LOOK BACK AND AHEAD.

Part I

In the first part of the book you learned that the use of paint is to save expense and loss, and look nice; that it pays to paint as soon as a building needs paint, and paint well.

Part II

In the second part, you learned that paint should turn water, continue to turn it year after year, that the way to have it turn water and to wear, is to make it of genuine stuff, not bogus; that bogus abounds; that paint should look nice too; must be cheap, as we commonly mean by cheap; and ought to be cheap by the year, which is over the heads of nine-tenths of people; that poverty comes of being misled by good-for-nothing "cheap."

Are you ready

Now you come to the heart of the book, what to do and not do, in getting your paint and putting it on. One thing at a time.

### LEAD AND OIL.

Public opinion

Lead and oil comes first, because it ranks first in public opinion. Public opinion, however, is never quite right; for it is the opinion of average men. We want the opinion of those who know all about it—it is the oldest of paints and perfectly known—and we want the opinion of those who also know what else there is in the world.

Lead and oil was the only available white, for about two hundred years. It was a good system—no doubt about that. But zinc has come into use. To call lead and oil the best to-day, because it was the best a hundred years ago, and is still approved by those who know little or nothing of zinc, is just like public opinion—always behind the times.

Zinc has come into use

There are millions of dollars invested in lead, naturally, doing all it can to keep up the old system of painting. Money invested in anything always resists a change from that thing; it is human nature. And these millions can do a great deal to maintain an established business.

Lead in use

Nevertheless, the consumption of lead in the United States is about 250,000 barrels against 325,000 barrels of zinc: about 75,000 more barrels of zinc than of lead. Notwithstanding this following pile of facts: (1) that lead is old and zinc is new; (2) that lead has a large active capital while zinc seems to have little money doing anything for it, may be it isn't necessary, may be it sells itself; (3) that lead has the advertising; (4) that the ancient custom of painters prevails, of saying, "I paint lead and oil"; (5) that the ancient opinion of people prevails, "lead and oil is the paint"; (6) that although more zinc is used than lead, the benefit goes to lead, and

Big odds

Zinc has won

zinc is apparently not much known or thought of—nevertheless more zinc than lead gets used!

We submit: This review of the progress of zinc, and decline of lead, bears hard on the question: which is the better system? With all the circumstances in favor of lead, zinc is winning the business; has won already more than half of it. Evidently lead and oil is not the best paint, and hasn't been, twenty or thirty years.

Paint record of twenty or thirty years

Let us see what has happened these twenty or thirty years in this country of ours. The country has doubled in people and wealth; and the business of painting has vastly more than doubled. As happens in sudden developments, much of the growth has been out of the usual lines. All trades have been pushed with excess of work; unapprenticed men have been employed to fill the demand; the standards of work have not altogether improved; men have taken to doing their own house-painting, etc., to some extent; and ready-made paints have been made by the many millions of gallons. These ready-made

Zinc in all readymade paints

paints are of all degrees of goodness and badness (and zinc is in most of them.)

Zinc in shop-mixed paints

Lead and oil has always been known to chalk off, to powder away: the outside wears out and goes off; in about three years in the best of jobs (lead and oil) the whole coat is more chalky than rubbery. Ready-made paints did not chalk off—may be zinc prevented the chalking. The painters tried a proportion of zinc with their lead and diminished the chalking. So they adopted zinc.

You see where the zinc goes, it goes into readymade paints and into painter-made paints also. And it does good service wherever it goes. It goes into readymade paints to harden the lead, keep it from chalking and therefore make the paint wear longer. It goes into shop-mixed paint, " lead and oil," because all good painters want their work to be sure of lasting three years. Lead and oil was a good-enough paint before zinc came in ; it is good enough yet, with the proper mixture of zinc. The standard is higher now. Lead and oil is surer to last three years than formerly ; it has been known to last several years in good condition. But that was a mixture with zinc. " Lead and oil " is only the name of it.

*You see where it goes, and why*

*The standard is higher now*

*The effect of zinc*

### LEAD AND OIL DIFFICULTIES.

The first difficulty is adulterations; which can all be avoided by getting supplies from the very best sources ; in no other way.

*Adulterations*

Linseed oil is sometimes adulterated, but there is no difficulty in getting it right, whether raw or boiled, if you insist on having it pure.

*Oil is adulterated*

Turpentine drier is often made with too much turpentine. This amounts to adulteration of oil.

*Excess of turpentine in the drier*

**"Pure Lead" ground in oil contains water**

What is called pure lead (ground in oil) is in most paint stores : it is pure except it often contains a little water. The water has not been put in, but was not dried out in the making. It does no harm except flatting* the paint in spots after it has been applied to your house. The amount of water is small. The reason for leaving it in, is the cost of drying it out.

Our lead contains no water. We dry it out.

**Pigments and colors in oil grossly adulterated**

Pigments and colors in oil are more than often adulterated. We do not mean that they cannot be got full-strength; they can. Our own are full-strength. There are colors in oil reduced to one-fifth of full strength by barytes,† and no one can tell them from colors full-strength without testing them. One-fifth lampblack mixed with four-fifths barytes, looks as black as all lampblack.

**A paint store keeps at least two grades of colors**

Paint-stores often keep two or more grades of colors in oil, one line with the maker's name on the label, the other with some fictitious name on the label. The colors bearing the maker's name are up to that maker's standard, whatever that is ; the ones with fictitious names are probably half to four-fifths barytes. The only use of barytes in colors is to adulterate.

**How do you know what grade you are buying**

---

* Flat means without gloss.
† Pronounced ba-ry-teez. It does no good. It is used in the place of the pigments because it is cheap.

Suppose you want a certain amount of a Example certain gray paint, and your formula calls for one pound of pure lampblack in oil. If your lampblack is 50 per cent. barytes you've got to put in 2 lbs.; if 60 per cent. barytes, 2½ lbs.; if 80 per cent. barytes, 5 lbs. You must know what strength your formula calls for and the strength of your color; then you can compute how much to buy for your job. Painters get over the difficulty by sticking to one brand— it may or may not be always alike.

Adulteration isn't confined to paint. There Another example is more demand for low prices than for anything else in the world, and the easiest way to make them is to adulterate. Pure milk is landed in New York at a cost of six cents a quart and is retailed at three to eight cents. The eight-cent milk is the cheapest, the three cent milk is the dearest and pays the most profit.

This is the way " close buyers " are served. They "like to be humbugged" There is no other way to do business, except so far as it is controlled by powerful makers, dealers and users, or by government—haven't yet got on so far as the latter in this country.

A paint-store keeps a small part of one Two or three sets of stuff in a store manufacturer's products; another store, in the same town, has a few of another maker's products. The goods of the two stores are called by the same names, but are different. A painter buys his supplies at one of the stores and learns how to use them by trying.

There may or may not be good goods in both stores.

Such are a painter's resources for making paint, and all his resources. If he is a man disposed to take risks, he says to himself: "the less my materials cost the more money I make," and he buys what is called cheap stuff. If he is a careful man, he uses the better grades. He is sure of his job when he uses his old. familiar materials only; whenever he uses anything new to him it is an ex-

periment. No wonder good painters are slow to try experiments.

Lead and oil, as a system you see, involves the difficulty of making paint, without knowing more than a few materials, and without facilities. There are doctors who know a dozen prescriptions and carry the stuff in a bag. They do their best, no doubt; but their best is rarely quite right.

## FACTORY-WORK.

In every kind of industry, factory-work is better or worse than home-made or small-shop-made; and, whether better or worse, it costs less money.

Factory-work is done on a large scale; all the knowledge, there is, is available for it; steam and machinery do the drudgery; even the labor employed is more of the mind than of body; the product is such as the maker chooses to make; the costs are low; and the lower the prices, the larger the output and profit. It is the progress of civilization in business.

*Civilization in business*

The making of paint is a good illustration of it. The best and worst paint are both made in great works, and made for less money than painters can make them for.

*Economical work*

What shall a painter do about it? Stating the question answers it. Evidently the making of paint no longer belongs to the work a painter can do to advantage.

*Don't try to compete with a factory*

## SECRET PAINTS.

For fifty years, the world has been increasingly full of secret paints and medicines. Some are better than others, of course; but one does not quite like to risk a paint or medicine made by a man in the dark.

*Apt to be quacks, of course*

There is a great deal of money in paint: we suppose $100,000,000 a year in the United States. A good deal of it goes for paint that nobody knows the materials of—many millions a year for bogus paint—and the worse it is, the shorter time it lasts, and the sooner the houses need painting again.

*Millions a year for bogus paint*

We have heard it said that the biggest part of the cost of a bottle of medicine is, sometimes, the bottle. Paint is made the same way. Of course, the maker don't tell what he makes it of.

*Why secret*

On the other hand, the easiest way to sell a good thing is to tell what it is. So, per-

*A quack is always secret*

haps, it is wise to buy paints that are made, by responsible makers, of known and approved materials. People generally have come to this conclusion.

## WHITE-LEAD.

Formerly lead was the only available white. It is still necessary, with zinc; but lead is no longer used, without zinc, by painters who know what is going on in the world.

The old stand-by still necessary

Lead alone does not wear well outdoors, and yellows or darkens indoors. But the bulk of people, with painting to do, want lead: they consider it genuine. They are afraid of anything else: they consider it spurious.

People haven't found out the importance of zinc

Lead, well put on, is good for about three years; and three years has come to be an established standard of wear. If owners are willing to paint again in three years, you can't blame painters, for doing the work, and talking about it, so as to get the job. So they mix enough zinc with their lead to make sure of its wearing three years, and say nothing about it.

Three years' wear satisfactory

A little zinc makes sure of that

We have before referred to the powerful influences, upon both painters and public, in favor of lead; but they are as nothing, compared with the pressure on painters, by owners, for lead. "Lead and oil is good enough for me" is a frequent expression with both. "Let a customer have what he

Let 'em have what they want

wants " is common shop wisdom. " If people want lead, let 'em have it, of course," is paint-shop wisdom. But painters are not very quick to get news about paint, and thousands of them actually have not yet found out the effect of zinc in lead paint. We shall get to that soon.

*Some painters don't know yet*

This chapter is headed " white-lead," but has run into painters' attitude towards it. Which couldn't be helped. White-lead doesn't mean white-lead any more; it is something to talk, not to paint.

*Talked about more than painted*

The use of lead, at the end of the nineteenth century, is: to mix with zinc. We shall have to return to the tactics about it, after a little.

*Modern use of lead*

### ZINC INDOORS.

In the common practice of painters nowadays, zinc is in general use indoors; because it is whiter than lead at its whitest, and stays white; while lead turns yellow or black.

*Whiter, unchangeable, holds colors better*

It is worth your while to notice the reason why lead undergoes a change in paint, and zinc does not, for its bearing on paint outdoors: it is chemical action. Lead is more ready than zinc to join in chemical action. Such action sets in between lead and colors and oil, and not between zinc and colors and oil. A little sulphur, that blackens lead paint, has no effect on zinc. There is sulphur enough evolved in the burning of gas, and sometimes in the gas that escapes

*Zinc constant, lead fickle*

from a stove or furnace, to blacken lead paint.
Neither sulphur, nor anything else, has any
effect on zinc paint.

Lead unstable, zinc stable

The cause of lead's chalking outdoors is
chemical action also; not the same. Both
cause and effect are different. Lead, being
rather disposed to chemical action, chalks off
outdoors and changes color indoors. The
weakness of lead is its chemical instability;
the strength of zinc is its stability.

ZINC OUTDOORS.

An extremely practical practical joke

About fifty years ago, a first-class house-
painter and business man, in Paris, adopted
zinc *on the sly*—professing to paint lead and
oil—and, his work was so good, he became the
leading painter of Paris. After a while he let

Pussy gets out

the cat out of the bag, and zinc became, to a
large extent, the accepted paint of France.

Pussy did it

If he had openly offered zinc as better than
lead, he would not have succeeded. The following bits of history make this clear.

Scientist failed

In 1781, a French chemist discovered the
use of zinc as a pigment, and advised its
use; nothing came of it.

Inventor failed

In 1796, an Englishman claimed some in-
vention with zinc as a pigment and got it
patented. This woke up the Frenchman; but
nothing came of it.

Manufacturer failed

In 1844, a Frenchman made zinc; and, in
1851, a French company made it. The com-

pany still survives as La Vieille Montagne Zinc Company.

But nothing came cf it all, till the wily painter established himself and zinc by his 'cute little trick: *painting zinc and getting it judged as lead.* Painter and pussy did it

His name was Leclair. He died in 1872; five years after his death, 984 workmen, employed by his firm, were profit-sharers with it. He left a moderate fortune, having preferred benevolence all his life. He received a gold medal from the Society for the Encouragement of the Arts and was decorated by the government, with the Grand Cross of the Legion of Honor, for having improved the practice of painters: i.e.: for that beautiful trick on his craft and customers. Leclair Redouly Valmé et Cie successors

Such is the history. Zinc was known as a pigment seventy years before it got into use. It got into use as "lead;" was approved as "lead;" won success and celebrity, first, as "lead;" then came to its own. Same in the United States, only slower

But this was all-zinc; and our painters agree that all-zinc will not stand out-doors: it is too hard: it is apt to crack and peel off. This seems at first to put doubt on the tale; but, as often happens, a little further inquiry explains the discrepancy. A discrepancy

We use linseed oil in paint. The French use poppy oil. It was zinc and poppy oil that Leclair won his victory with. One is about as good as the other perhaps; but lin- Linseed and poppy oils

seed dries harder than poppy, makes harder
paint. With linseed oil, we soften zinc by
adding sufficient lead.

*Poppy tempers zinc*

Do you remember? We said the modern
use of lead is to mix with zinc. That is
clearer now. We can't use poppy oil, because
our tariff makes it too costly. This illus-
trates another point: that paint must be
cheap. But, luckily, linseed oil and zinc, with
a little lead, appears to be as good a paint as
poppy and zinc, without any lead.

*Lead tempers zinc*

*French and American paint are about alike*

## LEAD AND ZINC.

It is abundantly clear, from the foregoing,
that lead and zinc is better than lead alone:
wears longer, is whiter, stays so, and holds
colors better.

*Better than lead*

The next question is: what proportions?
and next: how mix them? Is there any
better way than the painter's paddle and
tub?

*Particulars*

Some painters mix half lead and half zinc,
but, so far as we know their personal prac-
tices, few are inclined to use more than
twenty or thirty per cent. of zinc. We have
two sources of information as to the average
usage of painters: their buying supplies and
private talk with us and our agents; their
public talk at conventions.

*The practice of painters*

No other exposure is quite so hard on
paint as that at the seashore. Salt and sand
are destructive there; salt in damp weather;

*Hardest wear on paint*

and sand, when wind-storms drive it against the buildings, cuts paint, as a blast of sand cuts glass.*

For the lighthouse service the United States Government requires three-quarters zinc and one-quarter lead for white paint, which is enough lead to soften the zinc.

U. S. Lighthouse service

In making our ready-made paint, we have not changed our proportions for many years.

Our proportions

### SUCCESS OF ADULTERATED LEADS.

Return, a minute, to secret paints, to account for their very large sale, in spite of barytes and worse. And we ought to have had a chapter on secret leads—there are numerous brands of " lead " with fancy names, such as : *Lion Lead*, *Comet Lead*, etc. No one of these "leads" that bear such names — not the maker's name, not the actual maker's name— is actual lead. They are mixtures of lead and something else, and that something else is largely barytes — generally, not always. Adulterated leads are sold for less money than genuine leads. They have every other sign of discredit; but they have succeeded far beyond what is usual with adulterated goods.

Secret paints and

secret leads

All contain barytes

Some have been successful, nevertheless

The reason of these successes is that many of these irregular paints and leads yield better results in use, than regular leads. Lead

They deserved success

---

* Engraving on glass is done by sand blast. The sand cuts glass as a knife cuts wax.

and oil is the regular lead. All these off leads contain zinc; and the zinc is what saves them—some of them. Bogus is better than genuine lead when bogus is right and genuine wrong; and the bogus is so far right in containing zinc; and the "genuine lead" (pure lead) is wrong in containing no zinc.

Zinc explains the success of successful adulterated leads.

*Zinc was the saving of them*

*Bogus sometimes better than genuine*

*Zinc accounts for the wear*

## DEVOE LEAD AND ZINC.

*The material of it*

Our ready-made paint is named Devoe Lead and Zinc, and is made of dry white-lead and dry white-zinc ground together in linseed oil, and reduced by linseed oil to the thinness of paint. This forms the most durable paint now known. When the lead and zinc are thoroughly ground together in oil, and reduced by oil to the proper consistency, turpentine dryer and pure colors are added for tints.

## THE RIGHT MATERIALS.

*Importance of being right*

The Devoe materials—see last chapter for what they are—are right. The importance of their being right will appear from a few words on other materials commonly used in paint—next chapter.

*Rubbery coat with its root-like fibres extending into the wood is dried oil*

The object of paint is to form a rubbery coat on the wood. This coat is dried oil. A part of the oil soaks into the wood; a part remains on the surface. It dries and forms this rubbery coat, with root-like fibres extending into the wood. If this rubbery coat with its fibres extending into the wood and anchored there is perfect, the paint is perfect : water can't get through it.

The clinging strength of paint depends on this rubbery coat of dried oil, with its anchorage, also dried oil : entirely on oil : not at all on the pigment. The pigment only shelters the oil from wear outside, as sand and gravel and stones, in the bed of a stream, take the wear of the stream, from its actual bed. *The waterproof coat of oil*

The wear depends on oil and pigment : on oil alone underneath ; on oil and pigment outside. So long as the oil holds fast, the pigment is held to its work : as stones in a stream are held to the bottom by weight, and shingles are held on a roof by nails. And, so long as the pigment is there and is sound, the oil underneath is protected from water and wear. *is covered by shingle of pigment*

We could cheapen the oil two-thirds and the pigment three-quarters, and make a great deal of money—at first. The country is full of such paints and dealings. Or we could cheapen a little ; still make better paint than the average ; have more margin on it ; give dealers more profit ; put more expense on the selling ; and leave the way open for somebody else to make the best possible paint. *Thin coat and weak pigment*

We prefer the slower and surer course ; to make the best possible paint ourselves. *Best possible paint*

## ADULTERANTS.

The first thought about adulterants is: it costs twice the money to sell poor stuff: adulterations are dear. Adulterated paint is trebly expensive: costs more at first, not going so far; costs more by the year, wearing out so soon; costs more in damage to buildings—lets in water before you suspect it.

*Extravagant every way*

The worst adulteration of paint is by water.* Linseed oil will take in forty per cent. of water, with alkali. This makes soap; good-for-nothing in paint. The soap dries out and leaves the rubbery coat of oil too thin and poor; you painted mostly with soap and not much oil. The gloss soon goes; there may not be any gloss, in fact.

*Water the worst*

Petroleum also is used with linseed oil, in ready-made paints. The effect is about the same as that of water alone. It would never dry, itself; but an oil, that appears to dry, is made with petroleum. Does not really dry: in a week you can rub it off into dough-like crumbs with your finger. You can't dry kerosene; that's petroleum.

*Petroleum nearly as bad*

When lead and zinc are adulterated, it is simply cheating. But to adulterate linseed oil with water, petroleum and such things, and then use alkali to cover them up, is worse

*Simply cheating*

---

* It is an old saying that water and oil won't mix. Add an alkali and they will: but alkali kills the oil—turns it into soap. Women used to make soft soap by boiling together soap-grease and lye, and this lye is an alkali.

than highway robbery. It's like taking the wool out of your winter clothes and then trying to keep warm. Worse than highway robbery

Painters use too much turpentine. This may happen with any paint. If the weather is cold, the paint may be too stiff, and ought to be thinned a little. Gets thinned too much and too easily. "Turps" is altogether too tempting to painters. It does no good whatever outdoors; the less, the better. Three-and-a-half per cent. of turpentine dryer is all we use. That is necessary, and enough. To add more is an injury: it all dries out in a few hours, and leaves so much less oil: your rubbery coat is so much thinner and weaker. There is no way to do good work and use less oil. The more oil the better. Turpentine

Adulterated leads and paints are made of barytes,* whiting, china clay, terra alba and quartz, with enough lead and zinc to conceal Barytes, whiting, china clay, terra alba, quartz

---

* Barytes is the almost universal adulterant. You may like to know more about it.

When dry, or ground in oil with a little lead, it looks and feels like lead, and can't be distinguished from lead. It costs one-sixth as much. This is why it is used, in the main—another reason is stated below. It has two faults as a pigment.

First, it is so transparent, that, paint containing much barytes, requires an extra coat to "cover." The paint-maker saves perhaps $5 in making your paint and puts on the owner the cost of that extra coat, perhaps $60 for paint and labor.

Second, it saves oil—prevents the use of oil enough to form the durable rubbery coat—and limits the wear of the paint. *Barytes is used to adulterate pigments that cost even less than itself, because of its saving oil. The profit is made on the saving of oil.*

these things, which have weight and bulk, but no covering body. They are put in for weight when sold by the pound, and for bulk when sold by the gallon—to cheat. Enough lead and zinc is put in to present the appearance of paint in the package: to cheat.

No body

If you should paint with barytes, whiting, china clay, terra alba, or quartz, alone (without lead or zinc), you would paint a dozen coats *and not cover:* they have no covering property—are transparent.

Outrageous

Two-thirds of the weight of some "leads," and three-quarters of the bulk in some of the ready made paints, are of these adulterants.

Not so bad

On the other hand, as we said in a previous chapter, some adulterated leads are better than pure, and some adulterated paints are better than common painter's paint (lead and oil), because of the zinc they contain. You can't draw a line between pure and adulterated things, and call the pure things good, and the others not. Pure is not always good ; impure is not always bad ; and, besides, there are degrees of goodness and badness—in paints, as in everything else.

Colors in oil adulterated—why

Adulterated colors in oil we have treated in the chapter "Lead and Oil Difficulties ;" we ought to explain their existence here, though it is a digression. Our colors in oil are full-strength. They are sold all over the country, by one paint store in a small town, and by many stores in a large city: generally, of course, the best stores. These stores do not buy any other full-strength colors in oil. The only chance for another paint-material maker to deal with these stores is to sell them adulterated colors : they don't call them adulterated colors ; they call them "colors in oil." They sell for half or two-thirds or three-quarters our prices.

A painter goes to a store for colors; is offered ours at the price for ours,* whatever that is; and somebody else's for less. The only visible difference is: the name on the package. You know how easy it is to be taken in by a low price, and how many are taken in. It is the same in everything; everything sold is pure and adulterated, high and low-price. *Go by the name on the package*

Now come back to our subject a minute, which really is the effect of adulterants. *We are not wandering*

Suppose you are painting a house with some such paint as we have been talking about. It is said to be a "good paint"—all paints are "good" in stores—and "two coats will probably be enough." You pay $1.25 a gallon—eight gallons a coat—$10 a coat for the paint, and say $20 for putting it on. *Two examples out of your own experience*

* Very many merchants do not think it their business to influence people to buy good stuff and avoid poor stuff. They don't want to offend them by thrusting advice on them. You are supposed to know what you want. If you ask for his best, you get it. Show that you'll take cheap stuff, and you get that. Whatever you want, he wants to sell you exactly that; no persuasion about it.

He knows you and offers you best or middling or cheap, according to your habit of buying.

You get the two coats on: $60 for paint and labor. Looks good—new paint looks good—but you see the old paint through it. One more coat: $10 for paint; $20 for labor: $90.

The cost is $90

Paint another house like it—Devoe lead and zinc—$1.50 a gallon. Two coats at $12 a coat is $24 for paint; putting on two coats at $20 a coat is $40 for labor. Two coats are enough; and the cost is $64.

The cost is $64

This is not all. The house that cost $90 wants painting again in two or three years— the stuff may peel off in six months—but the house that cost $64 is good for several years.

The paint that costs less wears two or three times as long

We have shown you three ways of cheating in readymade paint: (1) by reducing the oil—we have shown you several ways of doing it; (2) by adulterating lead, zinc and colors—barytes, etc.; (3) short measure. The first is the worst; the last is least injurious. But, of course, a maker, who cheats in the measure, cheats in the other two ways besides; while many a maker adulterates oil and pigment, and covers his cheating, with the presumption of honest dealing, by giving full measure.

The three ways of cheating

You can't go by the price in the store, at all. The retail prices of readymade paints, as likely as not, are all alike: good, bad and indifferent: full-and-short-measure. Go by the name.

Go by the name on the package

## OUR PROPORTION RIGHT ENOUGH.

We grind lead and zinc together in oil, in their proper proportions.   We use enough lead to keep the zinc from cracking and peeling, and enough zinc to keep the lead from chalking—powdering off.

*Not exact*

We can't be sure that a little more lead and a little less zinc wouldn't be a trifle better or not quite so good.   The best possible mixture will never be known because all possible mixtures will never be tried on a large enough scale to establish results.

*Can't be*

The strongest argument, for the proportion we have adopted, is our experience with it. The next, so far as we can know, is that of the Government Lighthouse Service.

*The argument for it*

### SETTING UP A HIGHER STANDARD.

The standard of wear of paint accepted by painters is three years.   It has come down from the last generation; it may be older than that.   It came in this way.   Lead and oil, at its best, was good for about three years. When zinc became known to painters, they put enough of it into their paint to make sure of its lasting three years.   They tried to maintain the old standard, three years; and succeeded.

*The old standard*

We tried to cut loose from the old standard of wear altogether, and set up a new one, as high as possible.   We have succeeded too. We don't know how long we ought to say our

*The new standard*

paint wears.  We don't like to say six years:
we prefer to say twice as long as old-fashion
painter's paint, lead and oil.

## THE POLICY OF IT

**Cutting
the business
down to half**

Was it wise to cut the whole business of
paint-making down to half, by making a paint
to last twice as long?  Is it wise for a painter
to cut his whole business down to half, by
using a paint that lasts twice as long?

**We haven't done
that and you won't
do it**

There is a fallacy in both questions.  If
the whole business of making paint had been
in our hands, perhaps we shouldn't have been
so quick to reduce it to half; and, if the whole
business of painting your neighborhood is in
your hands, perhaps you had better keep on
with your three-years paint.

**Nobody else has
adopted our
standard yet**

Not so.  The business of making paint, in
the United States, was divided among about
50,000 makers by hand and 800 makers by
steam and machinery.  We could afford to

**which gives us
the business**

cut the whole business to half, to get our
share of that half.  And so of your neighborhood painting now.  It is divided among

**You, too, will find
your competitors
slow**

more painters than you can count; and you
can afford to cut your neighborhood painting
to half, to get your share of that half.

**Good work
is the best
advertisement**

Besides, improvement is in the air; and the
safest business is that which is quickest to
catch the improvements and get the benefit of
them.  The maker, who makes the best paint,
will have the most paint to make; and the

painter, whose job looks best and lasts longest, will have the most painting to do. There is great competition down at the bottom of everything: plenty of business and work at the top. And "top" means doing one's best for one's customer: we for ours, you for your's.

## GRINDING PAINT BY MACHINERY

Painters used to buy dry lead, and grind it in oil by hand; they had to; there was no lead, ground in oil, to be got in any other way. They ground it as well as they could, and bore the expense and inconvenience. They used to make their own varnishes also, as well as they could; and had to put up with what they could make. There was no such business as varnish-making, except the tramp with his kit. There was no such varnish, then, as is common now; and little was made. But now the business of varnish-making has come to great refinement and excellence; thanks to the man who makes a business of it. And, if anyone wants to know about varnish, the source of the knowledge is, not painters, not text-books or schools, but the factory. Writers of text-books, and teachers in schools, have no means of developing knowledge on technical subjects; the factory has.

Same way with paint. Do you imagine that grinders of paint by the thousand tons, with all the resources of science and steam and machinery, grind as painters used to with

*Old times in paint*

*and varnish*

*New times in varnish*

*Factory work is the same in paint*

boys and hand mills? By no means; if they set out to make cheap paint,they make it worse than a painter can; and, if they set out to make it good, they make it better than a painter can.

and costs but little But factory grinding costs very little. Machinery does an immense amount of work in a day, and requires attendance only. Materials, weighed and dumped in on an upper floor, come out below, a stream of perfect product. The work, a factory does, is far better than any a painter can do. The cheating is not in the work.

The process of grinding Consider the process of grinding lead and zinc. We mix, in a mixer, dry lead and zinc with oil enough for a paste, and grind the paste through a mill; then thin the paste with more oil to the thinness of paint, in a mixer, and grind the paint through a mill.

Mixing and grinding, too Our mixer mixes ten times as intimately as the painter's paddle; and the two grindings, first of the paste and then of the paint, not only reduces the pigments to powder, but carries the mixing to a degree of intimacy, in which the paint is almost as if it were made of one material.

Homogeneous paint There is a long hard word, that describes the effect of grinding: it makes the paint homogeneous: of one kind. Not merely one drop like another drop, but the millionth part of a drop like another millionth part of a drop: a millionth part of a drop is a uniform mixture of lead and zinc and oil.

You see how fine this grinding is: beyond seeing or feeling. The paint is of different nature from paint that is mixed with a stick. If kept some months in its package, the pigment settles and leaves the oil on top; but stirring restores it. The lead and zinc never part: the effect of the grinding is not impaired.

*produced by two grindings and mixings*

We grind your lead and your colors in oil; but most of you painters have so far done your own mixing. Of course, you don't trust us for your entire materials, and distrust us for finished paint: you haven't got round to it yet. We have helped your business by doing part of the work or making your paint; we shall help you more by doing the rest, when you are ready.

*You are used to this*

*not to this*

There is more money for you in varnish now, since we make it for you, than when you made it yourself. There is more money for you in paint, since we grind your colors and lead in oil. There will be still more, when we finish your paint.

*More money in it for you*

When you want a varnish for a particular use, you buy it from us by name. You know all about it—except what is in it and how it is made—you know how it works and wears: you know exactly what to expect of it.

*You buy varnish complete*

Why do you buy your varnish from us complete, and your paint three-quarters complete? The same motive exists for buying ready-made paint as for varnish. You know you

*Why buy paint three-quarters complete*

can't make varnish: you don't know you can't make paint. You don't know the im‑portance of grinding.

Effect of zinc ground in

Devoe lead and zinc wears twice as long as your paint. The reason is we use zinc and lead and grind them thoroughly together, which you can't do.

It affects the rubbery coat all through

We are artists' material-makers—every American artist uses our colors—we know what grinding is for. They formerly bought dry colors and oil, and ground them together on a slab with a muller. But we got their confidence years ago. We might say that we started at the top of the ladder. We started with the most critical people—the artists. There are no more critical people in the world than artists. We are now going to get the confidence of the painters—equally critical and difficult to please—but we feel certain of success.

When you see fresh paint, that is rough on the surface, you know it was not well ground; you go by the look and touch. We mean a thousand times finer than that. It affects the rubbery coat all through, and the wear of the paint: not the surface alone.

### GETTING YOUR TINTS.

Uniform colors cost you nothing

With Devoe lead and zinc you get your tints exact and uniform. All you've got to do is to stir it. One package the same as an‑other. Go by the color-card. Order your paint by the numbers against the colors.

Costs something
to get 'em by
mixing

Mixing your own, you know how hard it is to match samples. You may or may not know what colors, certainly not how much of a color, to use; you try a good many experiments. Quite a job to produce the tint you want; and, when you've got it, may be you know how you got it; and may be that's the best way to get it—probably not. Then if you find you haven't made quite enough for your job, can you make another batch to exactly match the first? You may take the easier way and mix by a formula. May be the color you get is good enough; may be it isn't.

and you
don't get 'em

## HOW DURABLE ARE THEY?

With Devoe lead and zinc, the tints last longer, because we use the right colors, because the paint lasts longer; they also last longer, because they are not affected by zinc as they are by lead; the less lead there is in the paint, the less the tints are affected by it; and grinding makes colors more durable.

More than in
other paint

## EASE OF PAINTING.

Devoe lead and zinc is about the same, as to flowing under the brush, as lead and oil: one tires the painter as much as the other: he doesn't know which he is painting.

Devoe
is easy enough

It seems a paltry subject for a chapter on house-painting: whether a paint is tiresome: the strain on your wrist. It isn't. We've

No paint that is
hard on the painter
could get into
general use

got to take the world as it is. If a paint is
hard on the painter, he don't like it, and won't
use it: he'll put turpentine in it. Good
painter or not, good man or not, it makes no
difference. Paint, to be used, must flow as
easy as usual under the brush.

## THE SKILL REQUIRED.

A painter may skip
if he wants to

We address the reader, as suits our pur-
pose, sometimes as a painter, sometimes as
owner, sometimes as both owner and painter—
amateur painter. Now, if you please, as
a home-made painter. But painters may
read—we rather like them to know what sort
of advice we give to a man, who is thinking
of doing his own painting.

Anybody can paint
on a pinch

He can do it; sometimes even women paint
their kitchen and bed-room floors. But they
find it a difficult, tedious and tiresome job;
and probably more appreciative of painters'
services afterward. Whether it pays, to do
your own painting, depends on circumstances.
If you have to do it, or do without it, of
course it pays; if not, set a painter at it.

It is not
so easy a job

Painting is delicate technical work, as well
as tiresome. Good painting will always be
done by experienced painters; bungling work
will always be done by the inexperienced—
painting as well as shoemaking. Painting is
not so easy a job, in either sense of the word,
as to tempt a man, especially woman, to do it
a second time.

We cannot supply the skill to do a good job, or the knack to make money by it. A man, who does his own painting, by no means saves all the money he keeps from his neighbor the painter; he pays himself, instead of the painter; but, if he reckons his time and strength and clothes, he may find he is working for lower wages than he would take from another employer for less disagreeable work.

Consider both sides of the question

There is, however, a great deal of painting done, where there is no painter; or, what amounts to the same thing, where there is no money to pay him. It is a great good to be able to paint your house, without the advantage of having a painter to do it. We give pretty full and exact instructions for doing the work on our color-card, and the paint in the keg or can is exactly right. You have only to see that the house and the weather are dry—you can manage the weather as well as anybody—and follow instructions.

But you can do it

Follow instructions

But people differ so much. You know how it is with boys: they like their own ways. You send a boy on an errand; he does it somehow, unless he forgets it. A man is worse than a boy: he "knows" so much more. We print most careful instructions for painting. May be you read them; may be you don't. May be you follow them; may be you "know how to paint" and don't. The boy forgot; which is right for a boy—he ought to forget

You know boys Do as they do not

a good deal that he hears. But you, with the printed instructions before you, don't dust or scrape the old paint, don't putty the nail holes and cracks, don't prime with plenty of oil and a little good paint, don't stir your paint enough or often enough, don't brush it out thin enough, don't wait long enough between coats, don't wait long enough for the water to dry out after a dew or fog or frost or rain, don't keep your paint and brushes clear of dust; and so, all through, you "know how to paint" and take your chances.

Follow
instructions You want to know what your chances are. We don't know, because we don't know the extent of your ignorance, where you imagine you know it all. It is like guessing what sort of a game of checkers a stranger will play. We go so far as this: we want our paint to make a good job wherever it goes; and we'd rather you'd leave it alone than monkey with it.

Follow
instructions What we have been talking about is will, not skill; but the usual disposition to have one's own way, in a matter he knows but little about, is much worse than a little awkwardness.

Will you do it One can do a fair job of painting without much skill, if he follows instructions.

### THE RISK OF A JOB.

This is for painters
but owners
may read it Nothing smoothes the way to a bargain like saying: "I'll take the risk of the job." You

often warrant a job to stand three years. A warrant ought to be something definite. What does it mean "to stand three years?" It is foggy now; in three years it will be much more so. The owner will be ashamed to complain of the job, in three years; and you will be likely to think it has stood three years.

We offer you something better to say than that. We have always had pretty close relations with painters: have made your materials. Now we propose still closer: *we take all risk of the paint.*

*We take all risk of the paint*

There are 50,000 of you, in the United States; do we mean to warrant the work of 50,000 strangers? No; but we take all risk of the *paint.* We can't expect to distinguish exactly between the risks that belong to the paint and those that belong to the work; we have to do more than we promise, or seem to be doing less sometimes. The only way to be just is to be a little generous. We are accustomed to taking the risk of your work in this way: if a job turns out good, it brings you business; if bad, you satisfy your customer somehow or lose not only his business but other business as well. When you mix your own paint, you take the risk of it, whether you mean to or not.

*You'd have to if we shouldn't*

If you paint Devoe Lead and Zinc you are protected by this:

*See how we do it*

" Send it to your State chemist; if he finds

it adulterated, we will pay his bill, and you $100."

You are also protected by this:

"If you have any fault to find with this paint either now in putting it on, or hereafter in the wear, tell your dealer about it. We authorize him to do what is right at our expense."

And "you" means painter or owner, whichever buys the paint.

See what a position this puts you in, Mr. Painter. You tell your customer: "I shall use Devoe lead and zinc, the best and most durable paint there is. You may buy it, or I will. The merchant who sells it (you call him by name, for he is your customer's neighbor as well as yours) is authorized by Devoe, in case of complaint, to do what is right at Devoe's expense—to settle the claim —not to send it off to New York and wait for reply—to settle it. That means cash. No, it don't. It means a good job. I shall do my part."

And see, Mr. Owner, what a position it puts you in. If you get a poor job, the man who bought the paint, whether you or your painter, says to the merchant, our agent, who sold it: "Here's a poor job of Devoe; I want what is right." And the merchant pays it. This happens sometimes. It is not an imaginary case. If the fault is clearly the painter's, the merchant refers you to him of course; if not, he asks : " How much, do you think, I owe you ?" Both sides are fair, and the case is settled.

It costs him nothing ; he has a good advertisement ; so have we. The probability is that the paint was perfect. We paid for the doubt. There is no reproach on anybody. You, who complained, and to whom a fault was acknowledged by paying damages, try it again. You believe, even more than before, in the maker and seller as well as the paint. The news gets about ; Devoe is the paint in your town. The people and painters all want it.

*No harm done to anyone*

*Good business all round*

Devoe lasts twice as long ; but more painting is done there than ever before, because standards are higher—people care more for the looks of their buildings. The town is richer, and shows it. See what a position we all are in. It costs us $10, $20, $50, may be $100, to pay your loss ; and we have every man in the town as a friend.

*More painting than ever for you*

*More business for us*

All this supposes that nobody tries to cheat. It is honest business all round. A rosy view. Our agent has got to look out for false claims, for his own protection as well as ours. When a job goes wrong, there is generally no difficulty in tracing the cause of its going wrong.

*We don't mean to fool away money*

It is nothing new, to warrant our paint : we have done it for years ; without getting the benefit of it, because we have done it privately.

*It is wisdom*

Still, we have done it enough to be able to say that it works as stated: it gives us the business wherever our system is known; and it is our own fault, if it isn't known everywhere.

### THE PAINTER'S INTEREST.

It makes you a businessman

Which would you rather do, Mr. Painter: buy lead, zinc, oil, turpentine dryer and colors; mix as you can; and take your chance? or buy Devoe, get exactly the tints your customer wants, get twice the wear, be safe yourself, and have your customer safe—for less money?

It makes you more of a business man than you used to be.

### OF ALL THE READYMADE PAINTS.

Only one is best in 800

Devoe is the one that is pure, full-measure and right. There are in the United States about eight-hundred paint manufacturers, making millions of gallons a year of paint of various grades, from thoroughly bad to thoroughly good.

Short-measure and adulterated

In some localities, they are all short measure as well as adulterated: in others, full measure and adulterated. What we mean by right is: made of the right materials. Wrong: of the wrong materials.

Devoe is full measure—measure it and satisfy yourself. Devoe is not adulterated. You can't prove this yourself, but a chemist can:

Here's the proof:

WILLIS G. TUCKER, M.D.,
    Professor of Inorganic and
    Analytical Chemistry.

CHEMICAL LABORATORY OF THE
ALBANY MEDICAL COLLEGE.

ALBANY, N. Y., Feb., 3d, 1899.

I have lately bought in the open market a sealed package of F. W. Devoe & Co.'s "Pure Lead & Zinc Paint," and have subjected it to a chemical analysis with the following results:

I find that the paint is made only of pure white lead (carbonate of lead), pure white zinc (oxide of zinc), pure linseed oil, pure turpentine dryer, and pure tinting colors.

The paint contains no adulteration in any form.

Signed,
WILLIS G. TUCKER, M.D.,
Prof. Inorg. and Analytical
Chemistry, Albany Medical
College.

*The above certificate of analysis was issued by Prof. Willis G. Tucker, Official Chemist to the State of New York.*

One of the best of these paints has barytes for lead—no lead in it—barytes and zinc. The barytes tempers the zinc, and the paint wears fairly well. It is the same as Devoe, except that it has barytes for lead. Two coats of this paint are exactly equal to one of Devoe. What a foolish business it is to make paint, that is otherwise good, but requires an extra coat! And yet that barytes and zinc is a more economical paint than the old lead and oil, because it wears longer.

*A strange business*

*No lead in it*

## PAINTING AND MAKING PAINT.

Your business

The business of painting belongs to painters, because they do it better than anybody else, and at fair prices. The business of

Our business

making paint belongs to us, because we do it better than anybody else, and at fair prices—less than painters can make lead and oil for, and for as little as other paint manufacturers make inferior paint for.

Common interest

This is the way to own a business : to do it better than anybody else, and at fair prices: so that your customers want you to own it.

### OUR TITLE TO CONFIDENCE.

An old, good name
to maintain

Our business began in 1754, and has continued without a break one-hundred and forty-five years. So far as we know, it is the oldest business in New York, and there are only four older businesses in the United States.

Our business
is valuable

It is the oldest, and has been, perhaps always, the largest business, in paints and varnishes, in the United States—we presume in the world.

We know our work

We have about all the resources there are in existence for making improvements, as may appear from two circumstances. We have, as customers, many concerns that use their own scientific and practical knowledge in buying supplies. We furnish the paint, for instance, for most of the railroad, steamer and lighthouse property.

All these things would afford but little assurance to painters and property-owners, if we were engrossed by large transactions and careless of small. We are not. We especially seek the trade of the better class of paint-stores all over the country.

We value the trade of the people

Devoe lead and zinc is pure. Whoever wants to be assured of the purity of it may send an original package to his State chemist for analysis. If found adulterated, we will pay the expense and $100 to the inquirer.

Devoe is pure

Whoever uses this paint, and finds it any-way short of his proper expectations, either at once in the painting or afterward in the wear, may go to the merchant, from whom he bought it, and get what the merchant considers due. We authorize him to pay it, without consulting us.

We insure satisfaction

Pay damages if there are any

www.ingramcontent.com/pod-product-compliance
Lightning Source LLC
Chambersburg PA
CBHW031752090426
42739CB00008B/975